101
Mom Jokes

Like dad jokes, only smarter.

By: Elias Hill

Illustrations By: Katherine Hogan

Elias Hill and Katherine Hogan
101 Mom Jokes
Copyright 2017

Tiny Camel Books
tinycamelbooks@gmail.com
www.tinycamelbooks.com

Cook a man a fish and you feed him for an hour.
Teach a man to fish, and you can get rid of him for an entire weekend!

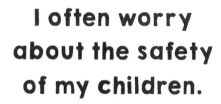

Never, ever ask a woman if she is pregnant unless you see an actual baby being born.

Even then, act surprised.

My son is shameless, inappropriate, naughty, and offensive.

In other words, he got my best qualities.

This past election was a tough one.

But once again I am president of the Messy Hair and Sweatpants Club.

I can't wait until I'm old enough

to pretend I can't hear.

If you have an opinion about how I should be raising my kids, please put your hand up.

Now cover your mouth.

What do IDK, LY & TTYL mean?

I don't know, love you, talk to you later.

Fine, I'll ask your brother then!

??

I will always love you when you hurt yourself...

unless you hurt yourself doing something stupid I told you not to. Then, well, you kind of deserve it.

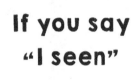

If you say
"I seen"

then I'll assume
your sentence
will never end
with "the inside
of a book."

Happiness is having a caring, loving and kind mother-in-law

in another state.

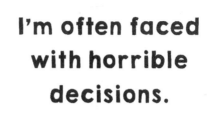

Messy hair,
don't care.

Retraction. I do care.
I care a lot. It's just
that motherhood has
required me to lower
my standards quite a
bit.

Teaching irony is important.

So when you yell "stop screaming" at screaming children it's totally OK.

Fun mom game-
take a drink
every time your
child whines.

Ha.
Just kidding.
You'd die.

I remember when naps

didn't give me that dry mouth, headachy, what year am I in, feeling.

Stop saying I'm hard to shop for.

Surely you know where the wine store is.

Am I getting older

or is the supermarket playing great music?

My husband acts like a boss.

Meaning he didn't do anything but he'll take all the credit.

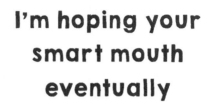

Hey, if you're going to kill each other...

do it outside, I just washed the floor.

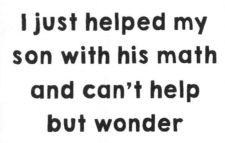

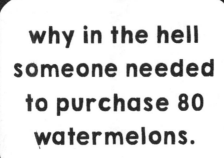

My mother-in-law needs to stop telling me how to raise my kids.

I married one of hers and he still needs a ton of work.

My parenting style has pretty much evolved into

"But did you DIE?"

Just when you think you can't go any crazier...

your kids come home with recorders playing "Hot Cross Buns".

Please excuse the mess, my kids are making memories,

of me yelling at them to clean up the mess.

I asked to switch my seat on a plane because of a crying baby.

Apparently that's not allowed if it is yours.

My kids are always accusing me of having a favorite child.

Which is ridiculous because I don't like any of them.

Don't be ashamed of who you are.

That's a mom's job!

If they are
behaving they
are mine.

If not,
I'm just the nanny.

One of my great satisfactions is when my daughter complains
that she's cold after I had suggested she take a jacket.

Me waiting for my son to finish a story.

How I manage to keep my children alive...

and kill every houseplant is beyond me.

The more colors in a meal, the more healthy it is!

My dinners usually include six colors. Seven if you include the color burned.

I got an A on my biology test!

WTF!

Mom, why would you say that?

Doesn't that mean Well That's Fantastic?

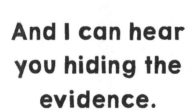